ideals®
CHRISTMAS

I wish you every blessing
this season can impart
and hope sweet Christmas finds you
with a carol in your heart.
—LUCILLE KING

IDEALS PUBLICATIONS
NASHVILLE, TENNESSEE

Signs of Christmas
Glenda Inman

Wreath of holly, mistletoe,
children playing in the snow,
carols sung by fireside glow—
these are signs of Christmas.

Yuletide trimmings on the street,
friendly smiles from folks you meet,
shopping trips and tired feet—
these are signs of Christmas.

Gifts all wrapped, the stockings hung,
every carol has been sung,
night descends, a church bell's rung—
these are signs of Christmas.

Children dozing through the night,
eager for the dawn's first light,
peace prevails and all is right—
these are signs of Christmas.

This Is Christmas!
Beth Edwards

Blazing hearths and drifting snow,
holly wreaths and mistletoe,
yuletide greetings, candle glow—
this is Christmas!

Festive trees and child's delight,
carols ringing through the night,
frosted panes aglow with light—
this is Christmas!

Presents stacked beneath the tree,
some for you and some for me.
But we cannot peek, you see—
this is Christmas!

Children's happy voices sing,
"Glory to the newborn King!"
while the church bells gaily ring.
This is Christmas!

Home they come from far and near,
those whom family ties hold dear;
laughing love and wholesome cheer—
this is Christmas!

Ancient tidings told again,
"Peace on earth, good will toward men!"
precious now as they were then—
this is Christmas!

*Photograph © Jumping Rocks
Photography/Gap Interior Images, Ltd.*

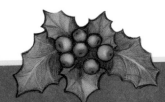

December

Harriet F. Blodgett

Holly branch and mistletoe
and Christmas chimes where'er we go
and stockings pinned up in a row—
these are thy gifts, December!

And if the year has made thee old
and silvered all thy locks of gold,
thy heart has never been a-cold
or known a fading ember.

The whole world is a Christmas tree,
and stars its many candles be.
Oh! sing a carol joyfully,
the year's great feast in keeping!

For once, on a December night,
an angel held a candle bright
and led three wise men by its light
to where a Child was sleeping.

Falling snow, mistletoe,
frosted panes, candy canes—
we've come to the best time of year.
Candlelight illumes the night.
Holly wreath, gifts beneath
a tree rising straight as a spear—
Christmas is finally here.
—KENTON K. SMITH

Christmas Tree

Edith W. Lawyer

In the cathedral of a forest
stood the tree, unadorned, serene—
with fragrant balsam branches outstretched
in welcome to her snow-powdered green.

Birds came to carol from her proud crown;
deer and hare played and slept at her feet;
from the velvet sky a star shone down
from the East, to make the scene complete.

Christmas Trees

LaVerne P. Larson

In the frosty winter northland
where the hardy fir trees grow,
there's a flurry of excitement
'neath the shawl of crystal snow.

The trees are oh-so-happy
when it is this time of year,
for they play a very special part
in bringing Christmas cheer.

It is the legend of the pines
and the wish of every tree
to stand in glowing splendor
and shine for all to see.

The spirit of the season
dwells in every evergreen,
and shines with glowing splendor
on the lovely Christmas scene.

Snowflakes Fall Softly

Keith H. Graham

A brown-eyed lad and a blue-eyed lass
press their noses against window glass.
They stare wide-eyed on Christmas Day
at scenes of the season on display.

Snowflakes fall softly,
floating on wisps of wind.
A blue spruce shows off royal robes
of diamond-studded white,
accented by a cardinal and the glow
from each reflecting light.

Snowflakes fall softly,
painting a masterpiece.
From icy trees a white-tailed buck
approaches, pauses, prances;
then hearing nearby window taps,
in his lively flight advances.

Snowflakes fall softly,
calling children to play.
Brother and sister run hand-in-hand
across their Creator's wonderland.
They chase daydreams under wintry skies
with glowing grins and twinkling eyes.

Snowflakes fall softly.

FAMILY TRADITION *by Geno Peoples. Image ©*
Geno Peoples/Hadley House Licensing

Family · Recipes

CRANBERRY-PINEAPPLE SALAD

2   3-ounce packages cherry or
      raspberry gelatin
1   20-ounce can crushed pineapple

1   14-ounce can whole berry cranberry sauce
1   apple, diced
⅔   cup chopped walnuts

In a large bowl, combine two gelatin powders; set aside. Drain pineapple, reserving juice. Set aside pineapple. Add enough cold water to juice to make 3 cups; pour into saucepan. Bring to boil. Remove from heat; add to dry gelatin mixes. Stir 2 minutes until completely dissolved. Stir in cranberry sauce. Refrigerate

1½ hours or until slightly thickened.

Reserve 1 tablespoon of pineapple for topping. Fold remaining pineapple, apples, and nuts into gelatin mixture. Refrigerate 4 hours or until firm. Top with reserved pineapple just before serving. Makes 12 to 14 servings.

BUTTERMILK MASHED POTATOES

3   pounds potatoes, peeled and cut into
      1½-inch cubes
½   cup milk
8   tablespoons unsalted butter

1   cup buttermilk
1   to 2 teaspoons salt
½   teaspoon black pepper

In a large pot, bring 4 quarts of salted water to a boil. Add potatoes and bring back to a boil. Reduce heat and simmer uncovered for 10 to 15 minutes, until potatoes fall apart easily when pierced with a fork. Drain potatoes and transfer to a large bowl. In a small saucepan,

heat milk and butter until butter is melted, taking care not to let it boil. Mash potatoes in bowl; whisk in milk mixture. Add enough buttermilk to make the potatoes creamy. Add 1 to 2 teaspoons salt and ½ teaspoon pepper, or to taste. Serve warm. Makes 4 to 6 servings.

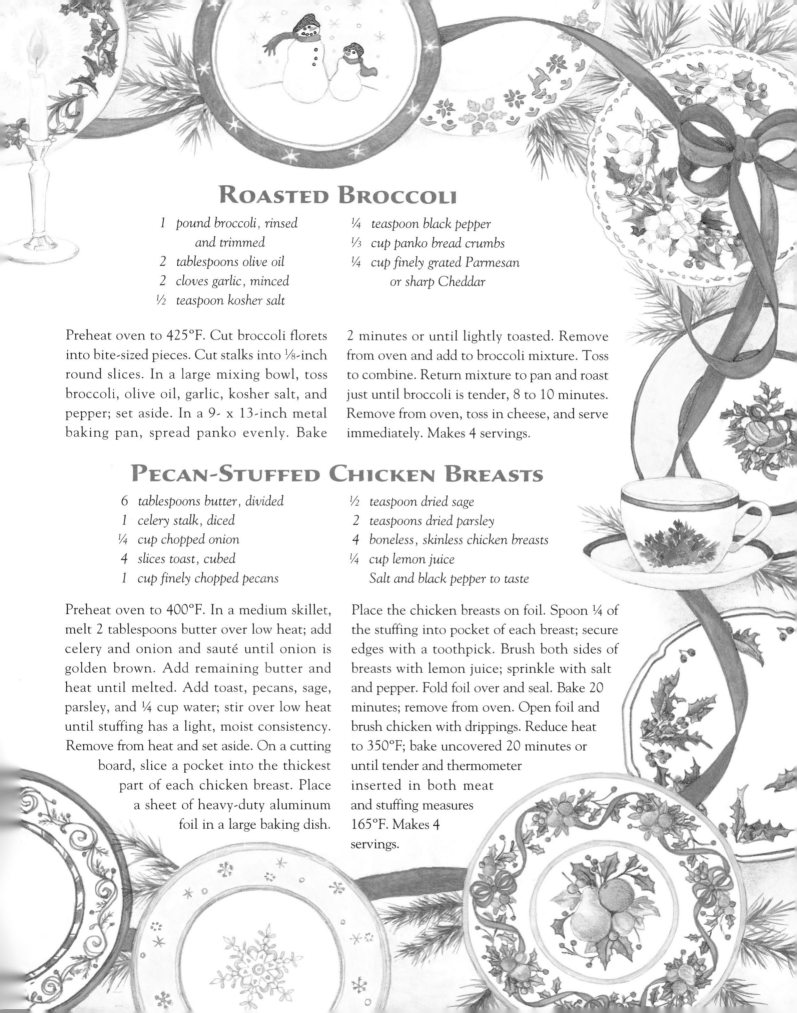

ROASTED BROCCOLI

1 pound broccoli, rinsed
   and trimmed
2 tablespoons olive oil
2 cloves garlic, minced
½ teaspoon kosher salt
¼ teaspoon black pepper
⅓ cup panko bread crumbs
¼ cup finely grated Parmesan
   or sharp Cheddar

Preheat oven to 425°F. Cut broccoli florets into bite-sized pieces. Cut stalks into ⅛-inch round slices. In a large mixing bowl, toss broccoli, olive oil, garlic, kosher salt, and pepper; set aside. In a 9- x 13-inch metal baking pan, spread panko evenly. Bake 2 minutes or until lightly toasted. Remove from oven and add to broccoli mixture. Toss to combine. Return mixture to pan and roast just until broccoli is tender, 8 to 10 minutes. Remove from oven, toss in cheese, and serve immediately. Makes 4 servings.

PECAN-STUFFED CHICKEN BREASTS

6 tablespoons butter, divided
1 celery stalk, diced
¼ cup chopped onion
4 slices toast, cubed
1 cup finely chopped pecans
½ teaspoon dried sage
2 teaspoons dried parsley
4 boneless, skinless chicken breasts
¼ cup lemon juice
  Salt and black pepper to taste

Preheat oven to 400°F. In a medium skillet, melt 2 tablespoons butter over low heat; add celery and onion and sauté until onion is golden brown. Add remaining butter and heat until melted. Add toast, pecans, sage, parsley, and ¼ cup water; stir over low heat until stuffing has a light, moist consistency. Remove from heat and set aside. On a cutting board, slice a pocket into the thickest part of each chicken breast. Place a sheet of heavy-duty aluminum foil in a large baking dish. Place the chicken breasts on foil. Spoon ¼ of the stuffing into pocket of each breast; secure edges with a toothpick. Brush both sides of breasts with lemon juice; sprinkle with salt and pepper. Fold foil over and seal. Bake 20 minutes; remove from oven. Open foil and brush chicken with drippings. Reduce heat to 350°F; bake uncovered 20 minutes or until tender and thermometer inserted in both meat and stuffing measures 165°F. Makes 4 servings.

A MICHIGAN CHRISTMAS

Joan Donaldson

This morning my family awoke to the silence of snow-capped pine branches and thousands of glittering crystals. The ground is covered with several inches of pristine snow. This is a perfect day for hauling our Christmas evergreens home on sleds.

The four of us set off. My husband, John, carries his wooden handle loppers, while the blade of a shovel rests on my shoulder. With their hands snug in wool mittens and stocking caps tugged over their ears, our sons drag their sleds. Our boots swoosh through the fresh powder that sifted from low-slung clouds drifting over Lake Michigan during the night.

We trudge across the pasture, while our three goats watch us from their little side door on the barn. Their breath puffs from their noses, and the bells on their collars tinkle as they walk into the paddock for a better view of us.

Our boys race each other as we head toward the hedgerows of pine and Douglas fir that border the pasture. John and I planted these evergreens almost twenty years ago when he built our house. That bouquet of seedlings has become a fan of fifteen-foot tall trees, stretching from the edge of the field to our pond. Some have dropped pinecones, and now baby pines rise from the needle-covered earth.

"Look for a small tree that you would like to dig up," I say to the boys. They drop the ropes to their sleds and slip through the feathery branches to begin their search.

The fragrance of pine swirls around us as John cuts off low branches and I stack them on a sled. From the firs, I select a pocketful of thimble-size cones. These are our cat's favorite toy, and I know she will bat them beneath the sofa and under the bookcase, stopping only when tempted by a fresh catnip mouse.

"Do you think I've cut enough?" John asks.

"Hmm, just a few more," I reply.

"How about this tree?" our younger son calls.

John sinks in the shovel, slicing a wide circle around the tree's base. Finally, the roots loosen, and the three of them lift it onto the other sled.

We all tramp home, both boys pulling the sled with their tree, while John hauls our evergreens. At our front door, John lifts the pine into a waiting pot and settles it into a corner of our great room.

"Let me arrange the lights, and then it's all yours," John says. The boys open their box of ornaments and begin to organize them.

A hand-hewn beam extends across the center of the main room of our timber-framed home. Here we array our swags of evergreens. I often wonder what stories the beams of our house could tell us of past holidays celebrated in settlers' barns.

"You need another one near the west wall," I say and hand John a branch of fir. The branches crisscross along the beam; they are a wave of pungent needles dotted with fir cones.

Our advent wreath hangs on white ribbons from the floor joists that support the upstairs loft. Plumes of white pine drape the wooden base. Burgundy rosehips glow beside the puffs of baby's breath, and beeswax candles rise from the greenery. Tonight, when we light three candles, their fragrance will remind me of midnight Christmas Eve services at my grandparents' church and the wonder of walking out of the sanctuary and scanning the heavens for a blazing star.

The boys hang satin balls they decorated with rickrack and sequins onto their tree and loop a chain of red, blue, and yellow construction-paper links.

After John arranges the lights across the beam, I lift other ornaments from a tissue-paper-filled box. In addition to the boys' ornaments, our others display the talents and affections of friends. John positions a red felt cardinal in the middle of the greenery, as our cat swishes her tail, wondering how that bird flew up onto the beam. I then offer John those ornaments given yearly by our friend, Jo, who has cross-stitched small rectangles or folded calico into stars. She slipped these gifts into the envelopes with her Christmas cards, and each one reminds me of her and the days we spent together in college.

I search the tissue paper until I find an English walnut wrapped in foil, fashioned by my hands at age three during Sunday school. This memento has endured almost half a century and stirs memories of singing in the youth choir

Photograph © Imagine IT/Shutterstock

while wearing a white robe with a green bow that tickled my chin.

Finally the box is empty, and John positions a translucent globe etched with an angel near a golden light bulb.

"Shall we turn on the lights?" John asks.

The boys have the honor of plugging in the lights. A spiral of red and blue, green and yellow sparkles around the tree, and the satin balls shimmer. Overhead white stars glitter along the beam, illuminating the white angels and their trumpets and the wooden rosettes John crafted on Christmas Day in years past. The assorted stars and angels, a paper-cut rabbit, and a clay goat—each ornament is unique, like the friend or family member who created it and whose love sweetens the holiday season of our lives.

Recipe for Christmas

Joanna Fuchs

Take a heap of childlike wonder
that opens up our eyes
to the unexpected gifts in life—
each day a sweet surprise.
Mix in fond appreciation
for the people whom we know;
like festive Christmas candles,
each one has a special glow.
Add some giggles and some laughter,
a dash of Christmas food—
amazing how a piece of pie
improves our attitude!
Stir it all with human kindness;
wrap it up in love and peace;
decorate with optimism, and
our joy will never cease.
If we use this healthy recipe,
we know we will remember
to be in the Christmas spirit
even when it's not December.

Holly and Tinsel

Mary Lou Carney

Holly and tinsel and
shiny bright balls;
pageant rehearsals
and trips to the mall;
singing old carols in soft candlelight;
knowing the Christ-Child
was born on this night;
sweet giggled secrets that no one
can hear—
all these make Christmas
the best time of year!

Join the Caroling

Rowena Bastin Bennett

Come out and join the caroling,
good friends and neighbors jolly!
Across the candle-lighted snow,
a troop of singers we shall go
and stop 'neath magic mistletoe
    or laughing wreaths of holly,
to sing the songs of yesteryear,
that old and young delight to hear.

The snow will hush our eager feet,
and we shall fill the silent street
    with bursts of happy song,
that those who sleep may dream more sweet,
    because we pass along;
that those who wake true joy may take
in this our festive throng.

The hollow night will be our bowl,
    the wind, our wassail stinging;
good will flows forth from soul to soul
as underneath the stars we stroll
    exultant in our singing.

But when the chimes in yonder tower
give warning of the midnight hour,
the winding way we shall retrace
and, with a good-night's parting grace,
shall leave the frosty skies behind,
    and each a hearty welcome find
within the Yule-log's warm embrace.

Come out and join the caroling,
good friends and neighbors jolly—
come! let us wreathe the world in song
more brilliant than the holly!

CHRISTMAS CAROLERS *by Doug Knutson. Image © Doug Knutson*

What Makes a Happy Christmas?

Harriet Whipple

It's being home for Christmas
among the ones you love,
perhaps with snow upon the ground
and twinkling stars above.

It's the love for one another
that shines on every face
and each familiar object
in its customary place.

It's pleasant recollections
we all remember well
but enjoy again each Christmas
to listen to and tell.

It's smells that are enticing
and favorite food to eat;
cards in each delivery
from those we seldom meet.

It's special preparations
and thoughtful presents too;
the usual decorations
that mean so much to you.

It's singing carols together
with Christmas lights aglow
and meeting with the neighbors
and friends we used to know.

It's sharing joy and bounty
and hopes of peace on earth;
it's keeping Christ in Christmas
as we celebrate His birth.

Bits & Pieces

The joy of brightening other lives, bearing each other's burdens, easing each other's loads and supplanting empty hearts and lives with generous gifts becomes for us the magic of Christmas.
—*W.C. Jones*

So remember while December brings the only Christmas day, in the year let there be Christmas in the things you do and say. Wouldn't life be worth the living, wouldn't dreams be coming true if we kept the Christmas spirit all the whole year through?
—*Author Unknown*

The most splendid Christmas gift, the most marveled and magic, is the gift that has not yet been opened. Opaque behind the wrapping or winking foil, is a box full of possibilities.
—*Gregg Easterbrook*

Christmas! The very word brings joy to our hearts. No matter how we may dread the rush, the long Christmas lists for gifts and cards to be bought and given—when Christmas Day comes there is still the same warm feeling we had as children, the same warmth that enfolds our hearts and our homes.
—*Joan Winmill Brown*

The earth has grown old with its burden of care,
but at Christmas it always is young.
The heart of the jewel burns lustrous and fair,
and its soul full of music breaks forth on the air
when the song of the angels is sung.
—*Phillips Brooks*

The coming of Christmas brings peace for the soul,
love for the heart, and great joy for the whole
of all of our living and all of our way.
May these be the blessings you find Christmas Day!
—*Ann Lutz*

THE CHRISTMAS SONG

Deborah A. Bennett

The first snow falls late on Christmas Eve, my family fast asleep. The sky is glowing pink as I carry a few logs in for the fire. Across the street, the neighbor's Christmas tree casts tassled light out onto the now-snow-covered yard and in the limbs of cedar trees, swaying gently in the wind. Back inside my warm kitchen, my wind-red cheeks are only beginning to thaw out when, in the familiar old porcelain bowl, I begin to make the last of the sugar cookies—the very last chore before Christmas Day. Christmas carols keep me company as I work, though it's never quite Christmas for me until Nat King Cole sings "The Christmas Song" on the radio.

I stir the batter—golden in the bowl and smelling of sweet vanilla—by hand, three hundred strokes, just like Grandma Ruby used to do. Moonlight glows through the panes of the kitchen window every now and then, and church bells echo in the night. The cookies already in the oven join the other Christmas aromas: the pine garlands and wreaths, the baking cranberry and turkey, the spicy sage and cornbread stuffing, the nutmeg tinge of the sweet potato pies, the molasses baked beans, the apple pies and the four-layered chocolate and coconut cakes waiting by the Christmas cards with the Charlie Brown tree on the counter.

I adjust the red and green paper chains hanging on the wall, calling to mind the child who made them—a little girl with hair the color of autumn leaves and laughter like jingle bells. She took some of her first steps on this very floor. Here and there, snowflakes hang: white paper cutouts as big as supper plates, multicolored plastic beaded ones, and pipe-cleaner snowflakes, each one made by a niece or nephew or young cousin, now grown.

Tomorrow they will all be here, in body or spirit, standing around the kitchen island telling stories or sitting at the good table in the dining room nursing hot chocolates while watching the cat paw at the Christmas tree. Some will be lounging on the floor in the living room occupied with a loud and contentious board game. A baby will be passed around. Quiet games of dominoes and checkers will be played with a group of watchers judging each move. Gifts will be given and received—some timidly, some ravenously. We will end the day with rainbows of paper and crushed and shining ribbons and bows littering the floors, trying to decide whose turn it is this year to clean it all up.

But tonight, it's just me. As the last batch of cookies come out, I go to poke the embers in the fireplace and to stand in the middle of it all for one last look before the day: the majestic tree, its tinseled branches wide with light and ornaments, like the glass-blown hummingbirds and angels and the ragged cloth candy cane my sister made as a child; the Christmas stockings with our names sewn on, hanging from the hearth; the dishes on the coffee table, filled with ribbon candies, walnuts, pecans, and oranges as bright as the sun; and the crèche on the windowsill, in which we placed the holy Baby only an hour ago.

I lift a box from under the tree, wrapped red with a bright gold bow, and give it a shake before, with a smile rising, I return it to its place. Then I cast one last look out the frosted windows, maybe searching the sky for sleigh and reindeer. All is hushed, and I see the wreath laced with diamonds of snowflakes. The porch light casts long shadows and a golden glow out on the new-fallen snow, on the Christmas Eve snow, as "The Christmas Song" plays softly on the radio, just as it did last year, just as it will next year, and all the years to come.

Photograph © MilousSK/Shutterstock

Christmas Comes

Clay Harrison

Christmas comes on catlike feet, silently at night
while the anxious world is dreaming and everything turns white.
Christmas comes like a baby's cry in a stable long ago,
the night a new star rose above to shine on Him below.

It comes like Magi from the East following His star,
bearing gifts as we do now to worship from afar.
It comes when earth is troubled, when all is calm and bright,
warming hearts throughout the ages on earth's most holy night.

Christmas comes on wings of eagles to lift our spirits high,
while children dream of Santa Claus and reindeer that can fly.
Christmas comes because God loves us and sent to us His Son
that we might live forevermore—God bless us, everyone!

Christmas Is a Feeling

Nelle Hardgrove

Christmas is a feeling
felt deep within your heart;
a gentle, tender feeling
that always seems to start
wherever people gather
and speak in voices low
about the lowly manger
and that night so long ago.

For even with the presents,
the tree and ornaments,
the family and the feasting,
and the way the day is spent,
the feeling seems to linger
and make each moment dear,
as if the little Christ Child
were sweetly sleeping near.

Yes, Christmas is a feeling!
A hallowed, precious thing.
So open wide your heart-strings
and hear the angels sing!

KEEP IT SIMPLE

Jewell Johnson

It happened again this year at our family's Christmas celebration. Someone said, "Remember the year when Ann made our presents?" We laughed and reminisced of a Christmas thirty years ago.

That December, five-year-old Ann pouted, "I don't have any presents to give." For weeks, her older brothers and sisters with jobs and salaries had been coming home with packages of mysterious contents. "Don't you dare peek," they admonished as they stashed the bags in closets. Ann felt left out of the holiday excitement.

In an effort to console her, I said, "You could make gifts."

I didn't think Ann would take on the challenge, but I was wrong. She flew to her room and came back with a skein of yellow yarn, markers, and a bottle of Elmer's glue. Then she disappeared outside on the Arizona desert landscape. In half an hour she was back and announced, "I've got all my Christmas presents. It's a surprise."

On Christmas Eve, Ann's three brothers, two sisters, her dad, and I opened packages revealing rock people, complete with marker faces and yarn hair.

In the years that followed, family members received many gifts from Ann, all more costly than a rock. Yet, at our Christmas gatherings, we talk about the wonderful rock people she gave us that year.

Ann's simple gifts remind us of another gift, the one from God. No one paid much attention to Mary and Joseph as they searched through Bethlehem's crowded streets looking for a room. Only the shepherds took note of the Baby born in a stable. Centuries later, people don't talk about King Herod or Quirinius, the governor of Syria, or Caesar Augustus's census decree. But from countless pulpits we hear messages of the gift God gave us. Reverberating through malls and city streets are carols about God's blessed Son.

Keep Christmas simple, without frills—like Ann's gifts. Perhaps that's the way God intended the birthday of His Son to be celebrated.

Photograph © Friedrich Strauss/
Gap Photos, Ltd.

Special Christmas Gifts

Ardis Rittenhouse

Standing outside this frosty night
with snowflakes drifting down,
blanketing the rooftops
and the streets all over town,
I find quite unexpectedly
the gifts I'd like to send
to everyone I know and love,
family or friend:

the peace so still and quiet
that I breathe in gratefully
until I'm filled with wonder
and deep tranquility;

the warmth of neighbors' windows
that reflect the Yuletide joy,

reminding me of Bethlehem
and the birth of one small boy;

His love that reaches out to me
as church bells softly ring
and youthful voices touch the wind
as carolers start to sing.

It's beginning to snow harder;
but before I go inside,
may all I've seen tonight
find room enough to hide
beneath your tree and in your heart
along with happiness,
and may these very special gifts
your Christmas season bless.

A Christmas Blessing

Louise Weibert Sutton

May the light of His love
and the glow of His star
spread the brightness of Christmas
wherever you are,
and the songs of the angels
who once hovered near
tune your spirit to music
while Christmas is here.

May the joy of His presence
be with you today—
a treasure unending,
not passing away—

while the peace of the season
awaiting each heart
that turns to the manger
be yours from the start.

The gifts wrapped in tissue
forgotten will be
in the years just ahead,
great or small though they be;
but the gift God has given
from heaven above
in the form of our Savior
is unfading love.

The Best Christmas of All
Kristi J. West

On this quiet Christmas morn,
the dawn's about to break.
The children slumber in their beds;
I fight to stay awake.

In place of sleep was wrapping gifts,
but sleep can surely wait—
I'll trade it for the memories
we'll make this special date.

Right now I hear soft whispers
outside my bedroom door,

and little feet creep down the stairs—
so eager to explore.

Sweet cries of glee and laughter
fill our living room with joy,
and giggles of their pure delight
arise from each new toy.

I'm mindful with each passing year,
this time when they are small,
each Christmas Day is special,
yet this one's best of all.

The Best Morning
Peggy Mlcuch

This Christmas Day is dawning and
I hear them on the stair;
their slippered feet are scuffling and
their whispers fill the air.

They can't be sure they should be up;
they try no noise to make;
they listen softly at our door
to see if we're awake.

They're nudging one another now
to softly crack our door.

In answer, Father utters a
loud, deep, make-believe snore.

They wait for just a moment, while
their giggles conquer dread,
then rush into the bedroom
and pull us out of bed.

It's been this way each Christmas Day
since they were very small. . . .
No wonder we think Christmas is
the best morning of all!

Photograph © Dan Duchars/Gap Interior Images, Ltd.

THE ROOFTOP CHRISTMAS

Marjorie Holmes

It would be our first Christmas in the huge Victorian house we'd bought in Washington, D.C. "And now that we've got it painted inside and out," said my husband, Lynn, "let's decorate the outside from stem to stern for Christmas!"

I groaned. "Honey, I'm tired. Let's wait another year." All summer and well into the fall I'd been scraping, sanding, painting. The house had been in terrible condition; but it was cheap and enormous, on a big shady corner lot, next door to the Episcopal church and across the street from school. It was a lot of work, but well worth the effort. And now that the renovations were done, I didn't want to look at another paintbrush or hammer or sandscraper.

Lynn looked crestfallen, so I listened dutifully to his plans. "We can outline the gingerbready roofs, cupolas, and porches with colored lights . . . put up some silhouettes," he said thoughtfully. "I found some old linoleum rugs in the attic, and all you have to do," he assured me, "is draw the figures on them." I still wasn't convinced.

"Make Santa and his reindeer!" our six-year-old chimed in.

"No," my husband said firmly. "I think Christmas should be Christian." He turned to me. "Don't you?" Then, ignoring my silence, "How about some wise men riding camels? . . . I'll cut them out and set them up; it shouldn't be much work for you at all. Of course, if you really mind. . . ."

I did. Art had been my second major in college; it shouldn't be too hard just to draw the things. But I knew from experience how impossible it would be to keep from getting involved. And I was indeed tired—Christmas or not. Meanwhile, the family eagerly went trooping to the attic to undertake the project without me. I hated myself for being a killjoy. "Well, I can draw pretty good," one child was saying.

I just couldn't stand it. I got up and went trudging after them.

They were already unrolling and measuring the stiff, worn rugs. Quietly I slipped into a corner and sat down with a bunch of old Christmas cards, looking for models, ideas. The unfinished wood of the attic smelled sweet—like a barn—and gradually a tender excitement began to build in me, the first stirrings of the Christmas spirit.

"Okay," I called. "How big do you want your camels?"

They turned in surprise and came running to hug me. "Life-size," my husband said. "It's a big roof."

Before the day was over, I had roughed out patterns on long rolls of wrapping paper. Lynn cut out the figures with a linoleum knife, and braced them, dark side out, with pieces of lath. By nightfall, backed by amber lights, three wise men rode out in silent splendor toward the scalloped balcony at the front of the house—the perfect place for a manger scene, I realized as I looked up, awed at what we had wrought.

Now it was my husband who protested, "That'll mean more rugs."

"Then find them," I laughed.

And he did—he and the boys—at a second-hand store.

So, next was Mary and Joseph, bent in tender silhouette above their baby in the manger. And we couldn't stop now—we had to have the shepherds, too, on another rooftop, leading or carrying their sheep toward the miracle the angels had promised.

And oh, how beautiful it was when it was finally finished. You could see them for blocks . . . the silent, radiant figures telling again the story of God's love for the world. I'll never forget how the church bells called us to midnight services that first Christmas Eve in Washington. And how people were drawn to our house afterward, inspired by that majestic rooftop Christmas scene. Some even came up the steps and joined us for coffee. New friends were made. Strangers driving by noticed it and told others. People across the city made pilgrimages to see it.

It became a tradition. Every year people looked for our rooftop pageantry. Occasionally they stopped or telephoned or wrote us letters.

"Hey, Mom, this is wonderful," said my son, now a teenager. He read aloud to me one of a stack of letters we had just received.

"'I'm a waitress. I have to work on Christmas Eve, but driving to and from work I go a few blocks out of my way to see your display. I can't say I'm a believer, but at Christmas when I see your house, I feel so good. And driving home after work, even if your lights are out, I still know they're there. It's sort of like they're watching

FULL MOON *by Richard Telford. Image © Richard Telford/DDFA.com*

over me. Well, I just want you to know and to say thank you.'"

My son grinned at me. "And to think you didn't even want to do it."

"Good heavens, do you remember that? It was years ago."

"I don't think any of us will ever forget, Mom. And when I'm married and have a family I hope I find a house with an attic and old linoleum rugs!"

"I hope so too," I told him. And thinking back to that long-ago afternoon in the attic, I said, "and I hope your reluctant family member can discover the joy that I have."

For I know now that the symbols of Christmas are so much more than decoration. They can be shining strands that bind a family close. They can be the chain of continuity for future families. And, illumined, God Himself sometimes uses them to light the way for strangers.

Silent Stand the Candles
Pamela Love

Silent stand the candles tall
with fragrant fir beneath,
shaped with care into a ring
to form an Advent wreath.

Weeks go past; by Christmas Eve
this circle evergreen
is topped by flame-tipped candles—
short, tall, and in-between.

Raise your voices, everyone;
sing of a Babe so small;
bright candlelight reminds us
He was the greatest Light of all.

Candlelight
Joy Belle Burgess

How far the Christmas candle
throws its beams of yellow light
across the silent snowdrifts
and through the darkest night!

The warm and friendly beacon
lights a pathway through the snow
and quietly shows strangers
the way that they should go.

The brightly glowing candle
beams a message of good cheer.
Within its golden burning
shines a welcome far and near.

What a comfort to the stranger!
What a blessed, cheering sight
to gaze upon the beauty
of a window warm with candlelight!

Photograph © Friedrich Strauss/Gap Photos, Ltd.

WILL THE CHRIST CHILD COME?

Gaye Jones Willis

One evening, about halfway through December, my family heard a knock at the door. We opened it to find a small package with a beautiful ceramic lamb inside. We looked at the calendar and realized that the twelve days of Christmas were beginning. The next night, when a matching shepherd arrived, we realized that the lamb was part of a Nativity set.

Each night we grew more excited to see what piece we would receive. The children attempted to catch the givers in the act, but were unsuccessful. Each piece was exquisite, and as we slowly built the scene at the manger, our family's focus shifted more and more to Christ's birth.

On Christmas Eve, all the pieces, with the notable exception of the Baby Jesus, had arrived. My twelve-year-old son really wanted to catch our benefactors and began to devise all kinds of ways to trap them. He ate dinner in the minivan, watching and waiting, but no one came. We called him in for our family's Christmas Eve traditions, and before the kids went to bed, we checked the front step. But there was no Baby Jesus. We began to worry that my son had scared them off or that they dropped the Jesus and there wouldn't be anything coming. I checked the doorstep one last time before I went to bed, but again found nothing.

Our family's Christmas morning custom is to allow the kids to open their stockings when they wake, but presents must wait until their dad wakes up. One by one, as they awoke, each child checked to see if perhaps during the night the Baby Jesus had arrived—before they even opened their stockings.

Missing that piece of the set seemed to have an odd effect on our family. It certainly changed my focus. I knew there were presents under the tree for me, and I was excited to watch the children open their gifts, but first on my mind was the feeling of waiting for the ceramic Christ Child. We had opened just about all of the presents when one of the children found one more for me buried deep beneath the limbs of the tree.

He handed me a small package from a longtime friend from our church. Over the years, as we spent time together in service and fellowship, I had observed that she and her family usually didn't have much for Christmas. Because it sounded like she didn't get many gifts, as her family chose to focus on their children, I had always given her a small package—not much, but something for her to open.

So the day before Christmas at church, when she had given me this small package saying it was just a token of her love and appreciation, I was touched. As I took off the bow, I was filled with gratitude for her friendship and her kindness in giving me this gift. But as the paper fell away, I began to tremble and cry. There in the small brown box was the Baby Jesus! He had come!

On that Christmas Day, I realized that Christ may come into our lives in unexpected ways. The spirit of Christ comes into our hearts

Photograph © William Sutton/DanitaDelimont.com

as we serve one another. As a family, we had waited and watched for the tiny ceramic version of Him to come, expecting the dramatic "knock at the door and scurrying of feet," but He came in a small, simple package that represented service, friendship, gratitude, and love.

This experience taught me that the beginning of the true spirit of Christmas comes as we open our hearts and actively focus on the Savior. We will most likely find Him in the small and simple acts of love, friendship, and service that we give to each other. This Christmas, I want to feel again the joy of knowing that Christ is in our home. I want to focus on loving and serving. More than that, I want to open my heart to Him all year that I may see Him again.

Familiar Faces

Pamela Love

I greet familiar faces
around this time of year.
Not just friends and family—
there are others I hold dear.

I keep them in a cardboard box
I bring out each December.
As I set up the manger scene,
I smile as I remember:

How my children played
    with them.
They chipped an angel's wing.
They asked the Wise Men
    questions,
and said the lamb should sing.

One year, they lost the camel,
then found him on the floor
being sniffed at by our puppy,
who wanted to play more.

And every Christmas morning,
by the tinsel and the trim,
they put the Baby in the crib,
and sang a hymn to Him.

The Christmas Silence

Margaret Deland

Hushed are the pigeons cooing low
on dusty rafters of the loft;
and mild-eyed oxen, breathing soft,
sleep on the fragrant hay below.

Dim shadows in the corner hide;
the glimmering lantern's rays are shed
where one small lamb just lifts his head,
then huddles 'gainst his mother's side.

Strange silence tingles in the air;
through the half-open door a bar

of light from one low-hanging star
touches a Baby's radiant hair.

No sound: the mother, kneeling, lays
her cheek against the little face.
Oh human love! Oh heavenly grace!
'Tis yet in silence that she prays!

Ages of silence end tonight;
then to the long-expectant earth
glad angels come to greet His birth
in bursts of music, love, and light!

"I Bring You Tidings of Great Joy"

Llewelyn Evans

*"We have seen his star in the east,
and are come to worship him." —Matthew 2:2*

In this most glorious season of the year,
heaven leans close to mortal ear.
The moonlit trees,
the scented breeze,
wing peace on earth, good will to men.
In this uplifting moment, still and calm,
the loving heart reflects the Christmas charm.
The manger holds
all God unfolds,
His peace on earth, good will to men.

Featured Poet

In Bethlehem: Singing

Eileen Spinelli

Suddenly—
startling light
on the shepherds'
pebbled path.

Suddenly—
the tender scent
of hay,
a baby's breath.

Suddenly—
a world gone topsy
with wonder
in a village gathered
under angel-wing.

Who would not sing
on such a night
in startling light?

Who would not sing?

WINTER SLEIGH *by Jess Hager. Image © Jess Hager/The Ansada Group*

CHRISTMAS BABY

Pamela Kennedy

A year ago, just before Christmas, our first grandchild, Henry, was born. It was a blessed event in every sense of the word. Mother and father were together, there were no serious complications, and the baby was born healthy and strong.

We had been anticipating this arrival since soon after the parents first learned they were to be parents. Each week we got updates from an online source called "The Bump" telling us the approximate size of our impending grandchild using fruits and veggies as comparison points. For instance, at week seven, he was the size of a blueberry; week twenty-two, a papaya; week thirty-one, a pineapple; and so forth. That whole experience certainly changed how I look at a salad bar!

There were prenatal doctor visits and labor classes to hear about, as well as a veritable minefield of new baby issues to navigate: breast milk or formula, disposable or cloth diapers, cradle or crib. There were supplies to gather and equipment to purchase: car seat, stroller, changing table, and such. By the time little Henry arrived, we felt we had already been on quite a journey together. And when we first held him in our arms, it was as if we, not he, had come home.

Henry's birth caused me to ponder the very first Christmas Baby and what His parents (and grandparents) experienced. For sure, no one was giving them weekly updates on the size of their unborn baby! Their prenatal plan probably involved casual conversations around the village well wherein the local mothers and grandmothers shared experiences, advice, and old wives' tales. As far as amassing large numbers of infant accoutrements, I suspect there weren't many options—maybe a few swaddling clothes and some kind of carrying device, perhaps a rectangular cloth to be used as a sling. This, no doubt, put a real damper on the baby shower gift registry business in Galilee. On the upside, however, since diapers and baby bottles are both relatively modern inventions, Mary most certainly wasn't bothered with defending her choices about either. And what about travel restrictions concerning expectant mothers in their ninth month? Good thing they had a donkey!

Then there was the birth itself. No midwives or doctors got called in to consult on the delivery of Jesus. Forget about fetal monitors and epidurals! By modern standards of sanitation, things were dicey too. No one was putting masks on the livestock or sterilizing the hay in the manger. And what about those grimy unwashed shepherds fresh from the fields? Holy hand sanitizer!

After spending a couple of weeks with our new grandson and his parents shortly after his birth, I have a new respect for Mary and Joseph.

They made it through Jesus' birth and first days of parenting with little help and few resources. Oh, I know the carol says, "The little Lord Jesus, no crying He makes." But that was written by a guy in the 19th century who obviously had never experienced life with a newborn—divine or otherwise! My sense of it is that there was plenty of crying, lots of wondering, and an abundance of uncertainty. I hope some shirttail relatives from Bethlehem took them in. Perhaps a granny who lived around the corner from the inn opened her home to the young family, gave the parents a good, home-cooked meal, a clean bed to sleep in, and offered to rock the Baby for a while. I'm certain that Mary, being young and far from home, would have appreciated that.

All in all, it is clear that Christmas babies are special blessings, whether they are born in a stable or in a maternity ward, with doctors and midwives present or surrounded by shepherds and angels. When we hold them close to our hearts and look into their infant eyes we see eternity reflected. And somehow we know that this is how God still communicates. This is the thread of love weaving generations together in common hopes and struggles. What a privilege to be in the presence of such a child and to understand again what it means to belong to the family of God!

The Light to Come

FOR UNTO US A CHILD IS BORN, UNTO us a son is given: and the government shall be upon his shoulder: and his name shall be called Wonderful, Counsellor, The mighty God, The everlasting Father, The Prince of Peace. Of the increase of his government and peace there shall be no end, upon the throne of David, and upon his kingdom, to order it, and to establish it with judgment and with justice from henceforth even for ever. The zeal of the LORD of hosts will perform this.

—ISAIAH 9:6–7

BUT THOU, BETHLEHEM EPHRATAH, though thou be little among the thousands of Judah, yet out of thee shall he come forth unto me that is to be ruler in Israel; whose goings forth have been from of old, from everlasting.

—MICAH 5:2

AND THERE SHALL COME FORTH a rod out of the stem of Jesse, and a Branch shall grow out of his roots: And the spirit of the LORD shall rest upon him, the spirit of wisdom and understanding, the spirit of counsel and might, the spirit of knowledge and of the fear of the LORD.

—ISAIAH 11:1–2

The True Light

IN THE BEGINNING WAS THE WORD, and the Word was with God, and the Word was God. The same was in the beginning with God. All things were made by him; and without him was not any thing made that was made.

In him was life; and the life was the light of men. And the light shineth in darkness; and the darkness comprehended it not.

There was a man sent from God, whose name was John. The same came for a witness, to bear witness of the Light, that all men through him might believe. He was not that Light, but was sent to bear witness of that Light.

That was the true Light, which lighteth every man that cometh into the world. He was in the world, and the world was made by him, and the world knew him not. He came unto his own, and his own received him not.

But as many as received him, to them gave he power to become the sons of God, even to them that believe on his name: Which were born, not of blood, nor of the will of the flesh, nor of the will of man, but of God.

And the Word was made flesh, and dwelt among us, (and we beheld his glory, the glory as of the only begotten of the Father,) full of grace and truth.

—JOHN 1:1–14

MARY AND JOSEPH *by Gordon Lees. Image © Gordon Lees/DDFA.com*

The Light of the Star

NOW WHEN JESUS WAS BORN in Bethlehem of Judaea in the days of Herod the king, behold, there came wise men from the east to Jerusalem, Saying, Where is he that is born King of the Jews? for we have seen his star in the east, and are come to worship him.

When Herod the king had heard these things, he was troubled, and all Jerusalem with him. And when he had gathered all the chief priests and scribes of the people together, he demanded of them where Christ should be born.

And they said unto him, In Bethlehem of Judaea: for thus it is written by the prophet, And thou Bethlehem, in the land of Juda, art not the least among the princes of Juda: for out of thee shall come a Governor, that shall rule my people Israel.

Then Herod, when he had privily called the wise men, enquired of them diligently what time the star appeared. And he sent them to Bethlehem, and said, Go and search diligently for the young child; and when ye have found him, bring me word again, that I may come and worship him also.

When they had heard the king, they departed; and, lo, the star, which they saw in the east, went before them, till it came and stood over where the young child was.

When they saw the star, they rejoiced with exceeding great joy.

And when they were come into the house, they saw the young child with Mary his mother, and fell down, and worshipped him: and when they had opened their treasures, they presented unto him gifts; gold, and frankincense, and myrrh.

And being warned of God in a dream that they should not return to Herod, they departed into their own country another way.
— MATTHEW 2:1–12

A STAR OVER BETHLEHEM *by Gordon Lees. Image © Gordon Lees/DDFA.com*

The Story of a Song

CHRISTMAS LULLABY

Pamela Kennedy

This beloved carol is American in origin but was believed for years to have been composed by the father of the Protestant Reformation, Martin Luther. The erroneous attribution can be traced to a nineteenth-century composer, James Ramsey Murray from Andover, Massachusetts. In 1855, Murray discovered the anonymous lyrics of the first two verses in a Lutheran Sunday school book, set the words to an original melody, "Mueller," and titled the song "Luther's Cradle Hymn." Murray published it in his 1887 book, *Dainty Songs for Little Lads and Lasses*, with the following note: "Composed by Martin Luther for his children, and still sung by German mothers to their little ones." But music historians have determined this statement is most likely just wishful thinking on Murray's part.

Eight years after Murray published his composition, another well-known American composer of sacred music, William J. Kirkpatrick of Pennsylvania, created an alternative tune, "Cradle Song," for "Away in a Manger." A member of the Wharton Street Methodist Episcopal Church in Philadelphia, he was in constant demand as an accompanist for the choir, singing societies, and church programs. As his musical talents developed, Kirkpatrick changed his career from that of carpenter to composer, and in 1895 he published his alternate musical setting for "Away in a Manger." Today, in the United States, the lyrics are most often sung to Murray's melody, "Mueller." But it is Kirkpatrick's melody that is more popular in England and is frequently employed by a cappella cathedral choirs and Celtic soloists there. Sung to either melody, the beautiful words of this Christmas lullaby evoke images of the Nativity, the Babe in a manger, and soft starlight illuminating the sleeping Savior.

This lovely carol seems to touch both young and old with wistfulness and hope. Perhaps this is because as we sing its verses, we recall the innocence of children and glimpse, once again through childlike eyes, the simplicity of faith. Pondering the contented Baby in the manger, we are reminded of Jesus' response when His disciples inquired about who is greatest in God's kingdom:

"He [Jesus] called a little child and had him stand among them. And he said: 'I tell you the truth, unless you change and become like little children, you will never enter the kingdom of heaven. Therefore, whoever humbles himself like this child is the greatest in the kingdom of heaven. And whoever welcomes a little child like this in my name welcomes me'" (Matthew 18:2–5 NIV 1984).

Away in a Manger

Traditional lyrics, music for "Mueller" melody by James R. Murray

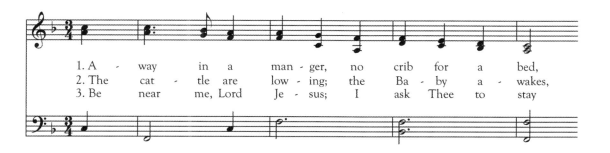

1. A - way in a man - ger, no crib for a bed,
2. The cat - tle are low - ing; the Ba - by a - wakes,
3. Be near me, Lord Je - sus; I ask Thee to stay

The lit - tle Lord Je - sus laid down His sweet head.
But lit - tle Lord Je - sus— no cry - ing He makes.
Close by me for - ev - er, and love me, I pray.

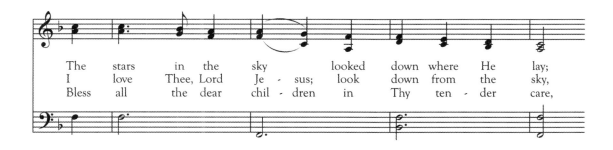

The stars in the sky looked down where He lay;
I love Thee, Lord Je - sus; look down from the sky,
Bless all the dear chil - dren in Thy ten - der care,

The lit - tle Lord Je - sus, a - sleep on the hay.
And stay by my cra - dle till morn - ing is nigh.
And fit us for heav - en, to live with Thee there.

God's Shepherd

Dr. Ralph F. Wilson

The frosts of forty winters had etched deep lines into the shepherd's face. Having spent his entire life outdoors on Bethlehem's hills, he was old at forty—and cold. The hillside where he sat this day was cold, too, and he pulled his mantle close about him to block the wind.

Every so often he would shift position, not as much out of discomfort as from a sense of unease, anxiety, *crowdedness*. Instead of hundreds of sheep with whom he felt quite at home, this hillside was flocked with people— thousands of them—listening attentively to the teacher. They could hear Him fairly well, except when the wind whisked away His words.

Tobias ben David was the shepherd's name, though people called him Toby. His flocks were in good hands this week, cared for by his grown sons, but Toby had left them to listen to Jesus of Nazareth. Today the teacher was talking about salvation, how God came to save His people from their waywardness and sins, to rescue them and gather them close.

Now Jesus' illustration turned to sheep. Toby felt better. He knew a lot more about sheep than people.

"The good shepherd," Jesus was saying, "lays down his life for the sheep. The hired hand who doesn't own the flock runs away when he sees the wolf coming, but not the good shepherd. . . ."

One night, years ago, the men Toby had hired to watch the flock with him fled when they saw a mountain lion roaming the hills. But Toby had

stayed. Shepherding was his livelihood. He knew the sacrifices that good shepherding required. He knew about defending defenseless lambs. He knew about putting his life on the line for the sheep. That's what good shepherds did.

Jesus continued, "Suppose you have 100 sheep and when night comes one is missing. What do you do? You leave the 99 sheep all safe together and then climb the hills, looking, searching until you find the lost sheep. Then you pick him up, put him on your shoulders, bring him down the hill to the camp, and ask your fellow shepherds to rejoice with you."

"Your heavenly Father is like that," Jesus said. "When you have lost your way, He will rescue you and save you and never give up on you until He finds you—and you find Him."

Toby's heart was racing. He felt a lump in his throat. He understood. Toby had combed the hills for lost sheep, not stopping, not quitting. He knew the joy of discovery, of rescuing the sheep from a thicket, of bringing it back and celebrating with his friends. He had been that kind of shepherd.

But he also knew how it felt to wander off, feeling lost, aimless, trapped. Clueless about where he was and where he was going. Flailing about, struggling to climb out of what seemed like a steep ravine. That's why he came today to hear the teacher, hoping to regain the faith he had felt as a child, a ten-year-old child.

His mind spun back to the evening of his tenth birthday. Like nearly every night, he was out on the hills with his dad or his uncles, caring for the sheep. The stars were brilliant, dancing in the black sky. But suddenly an overpowering bright light flooded the hillside. A voice boomed out, "Behold, I bring you good news of a great joy which shall be for all the people. For to you is born this day in the city of David a Savior, who is Christ the Lord!"

A Savior, a rescuer—shepherds' work. He had often wondered about the boy-child they discovered that night, lying in a manger, just as the angel had said. Toby had knelt down and worshipped the baby who bore the world's destiny upon His tiny shoulders. What had become of Him, this baby? By now He must be thirty-something. Had this Savior saved anyone yet? Rescued anyone? Could He rescue me from my aimless existence? Toby wondered.

Just then the wind caught Jesus' words and blew them in Toby's direction. "I am the Good Shepherd," Jesus was saying, "who lays down His life for the sheep. Come to Me, All you who are weary and heavy-laden, and I will give you rest. Take My yoke upon you and learn from Me," he said with warmth and joy full on His face. "For I am gentle and humble in heart, and you will find rest for your souls."

I wonder . . . thought Toby, as he felt big tears begin to roll down his cheeks and into his beard. *I wonder . . .* thought Toby, as joy and the certainty of God's love began to fill his heart. *I wonder,* thought Toby, *if this Jesus is the little baby I saw that night, the Savior of the world? Yes,* thought Toby, *He must be. His words found me and he sounds just like He's . . . God's Shepherd.*

Photograph © Elena Schweitzer/Shutterstock

Christmas Invitation

Edgar Daniel Kramer

Let us, too, wander with the star,
that leads us to the cattleshed,
where Wise Men, riding from afar,
and Shepherds come with
    eager tread
to heap their gifts of wool
    and myrrh
around the Christ Child's rosy feet,
while all the velvet shadows stir
to music mystically sweet.

Let us, too, heed the holy mirth,
that thrills across the starry skies,
that lifts the reaches of the earth
into the realms of Paradise,

while hosts of herald angels sing
in ecstasy to hill and glen,
"Unto the world is born a King!
God's peace on earth!
    Good will to men!"

Let us, too, kneel and humbly pray
to Him the hostel has denied,
while cattle munch their
    fragrant hay,
and, in His presence glorified,
we flout the doubtings and the fears,
we mock the dross of time and sense,
as we grow strong to face the years
with kindly Love's omnipotence.

Star of the East

Eugene Field

Star of the East, that long ago
brought wise men on their way
where angels singing to and fro,
the child of Bethlehem lay
above that Syrian hill afar
thou shinest out tonight, o star.

Star of the east, the night were drear
but for the tender grace
that with thy glory comes to cheer

earth's loneliest, darkest place
for by that charity we see
where there is hope for all and me.

Star of the East, show us the way
in wisdom undefiled
to seek that manger out and lay
our gifts before the child.
To bring our hearts and offer them
unto our King in Bethlehem!

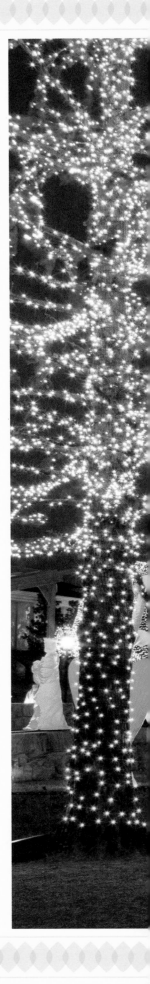

Photograph © Brian Jannsen/age fotostock/SuperStock

WHAT IS CHRISTMAS?

Sandy Cayman

Christmas, the holy day of love, of overwhelming happiness, of a joy so intense that the world reflects its glory to all the universe. Christmas, the living story of a miracle, of a truth that has survived the centuries. Tinseled trees shine forth in hope; faces glow in a radiance more lustrous than the crystal snow. Stars twinkle a bit brighter, and the velvet sky of midnight proclaims a splendor so magnificent that the very Soul of Heaven rings clear.

Christmas is more than just a day of wonder. It is a feeling of giving, of sharing, of remembering. Christmas must be felt, not purchased. It is warmth and friendship, grown closer. It is forgiveness and an even deeper faith in God and man. Christmas is adorned with holly and hearths; with bells and carols; with the family's abundant dinner, the expectation of presents for little ones and the elation of togetherness for their elders. Christmas is a symbol of all goodness, generosity, and kindness.

Christmas is a gift that has no equal, the everlasting Gift from God, that lived yesterday, lives today, and will live forever. Christmas, the holy miracle of Christ's birth, indeed the greatest story ever told.

Photograph © Jim Engelbrecht/
DanitaDelimont.com

Christmas Joy

J. Harold Gwynne

The angel herald spoke of joy—
God's gift to all mankind—
and humble shepherds quickly came
incarnate joy to find.

The wise men guided by the star
rejoiced with purest joy;
their journey led them where they found
the mother and her Boy!

And now this blessed Christmas joy
is known throughout the earth,
as joyful people everywhere
observe the Christ Child's birth.

And still the joy of Christmas comes
to fill our hearts with cheer;
this joy of which the angels sang
grows sweeter every year!

This Christmas joy within our hearts
is deep and full and free;
it is the Spirit of our Lord—
the Man of Galilee!

The Eternal One

Geo. H. Blanchard

I did not see the star that hung
o'er Bethlehem that night
nor meet the simple shepherds,
fear-filled by angels' light.

I did not hear the Virgin sing
her first low lullabye
nor catch the sound of trampling throng
that went unknowing by.

I did not bow to worship Him
who in the manger lay,
all bundled up in swaddling clothes
placed softly in the hay.

I did not see the seeking kings
who journeyed from afar,
with gold, and frankincense, and myrrh
led on by gleaming star.

No, all this happened long ago
as writ on pages fair
in ages past, ere I was born,
so I could not be there.

But ah, I know Him, know Him well,
and daily praises bring
to worship Him as lord of all
and crown Him as my King.

For He is the Eternal One—
Alpha, Omega He—
and He is mine, and I am His
through all eternity.

HARK! THE HERALD ANGELS STILL SING!

Rosalyn Hart Finch

Always, on the far horizons of the spirit, where all things are possible, soar the notes of angels' song, serving God and man alike.

Angels are referred to very often throughout the Bible in both the Old and New Testaments. But those Christmas angels who sang of exultation and reverence and love on that long ago Day of days, embellished themselves and their song indelibly on both the past and the future. And on the present.

This is the present, now, this Christmas season. It brings again the chance for us to begin anew, to reach beyond the narrow boundaries of self. A mystery of love as pure and forgiving as the baby boy, Jesus Christ, is a mystery stronger than life. We cannot explain it. We do not try. It is enough that on Christmas it swells triumphantly up and out of our greeds and prejudices. We leave behind, if only for a few fleeting hours, our dreary paths of cynicism and disdain and halt our aimless drifting toward self-indulgence.

We hard-pressed children of God who have lost track of the angels' song and keep mistaking the beacon of materialism for a star, suddenly strike it rich as we embrace the honest meaning of Christmas. Young or old, high or low, just or unjust, well or ill, wise or foolish—its miracle is again available for us all. Blessed are those ecstatic moments that fill us with gratitude to our Creator for His world and for the angels' song we share with His Son.

How sweet it is to hope, to love, to turn the other cheek, to feed the hungry, to protect the weak, to comfort those who weep, to forgive, to push back fear, to cherish children, to defend the persecuted. There are a hundred-million-and-one sweetnesses that pour out when the floodgates of the human heart are opened with love. So hallowed is the time that even those who do not seek Christmas are caught up in its exuberant embrace.

As we stumble through this world of transition, where everything changes but the angels' song, let us rejoice at this extra special dose of love—Christmas—that restores our fallow hearts.

Once again we can dare to live joyfully, live lovingly, live honorably and well. For the Herald Angels still sing, and we can listen!

Photograph © Bettina Salomon/Masterfile

Sing a Song of Christmas

Carice Williams

Sing a song of Christmas gladness everywhere,
snowflakes softly falling on the frosty air.

Sing a song of Christmas bells and mistletoe,
laughter gaily ringing, faces all aglow.

Sing a song of Christmas; hearts are warm with mirth.
All the world's rejoicing at our Savior's birth.

Sing a song of Christmas as the old year ends;
may the new bring blessings in the form of friends.

ISBN-13: 978-0-8249-1343-4

Published by Ideals Publications
A Guideposts Company
Nashville, Tennessee
www.idealsbooks.com

Publisher, Peggy Schaefer
Editor, Melinda L. R. Rumbaugh
Copy Editor, Debra Wright
Designer, Marisa Jackson
Permissions Editor, Kristi West

Cover: Photography © Nancy Matthews Photography
Inside front cover: Painting by Vickie Wade. Copyright © Vickie Wade/Good Salt
Inside back cover: *Cherished Traditions, Victorian Home,* and *Christmas Lights* by Linda Lovett. Copyright © Linda Lovett/Good Salt
Additional art credits: art for "Family Recipes" and "Bits & Pieces" and spot art on back cover, page 1, and page 52 by Kathy Rusynyk.
Art on pages 2 (© Sundra/Shutterstock), 14–15 (© elsyl/Shutterstock), 24–25 (© Abbie/Shutterstock and © Togataki/Shutterstock), 38 (© vitamasi/Shutterstock), 54 (© Natasha R. Graham/Shutterstock), 60 (© Heidrun Gellrich/Shutterstock), and 62 (© yuriy kulik) from Shutterstock.
"Away in a Manger" sheet music by Dick Torrans, Melode, Inc.

Readers are invited to submit original poetry and prose for possible use in future publications. Please send no more than four typed submissions to: Magazine Submissions, Ideals Publications, 2630 Elm Hill Pike, Suite 100, Nashville, Tennessee 37214. Manuscripts will be returned if a self-addressed stamped envelope is included.

ACKNOWLEDGMENTS:

CARNEY, MARY LOU. "Holly and Tinsel" from The Night the Stars Sang: A Christmas Celebration, copyright © 1965 by Guideposts. All rights reserved. Used by permission. FUCHS, JOANNA. "Recipe for Christmas All Year Long" copyright © Joanna Fuchs www.Poemsource.com. All rights reserved. Used by permission. HOLMES, MARJORIE. "The Rooftop Christmas" from Guideposts Family Christmas, copyright © 1980. All rights reserved. Used by permission. WILSON, RALPH F. "God's Shepherd" copyright © Ralph F. Wilson, pastor@joyfulheart.com. All rights reserved. Used by permission. OUR THANKS to the following authors or their heirs: Deborah A. Bennett, Rowena Bastin Bennett, Geo. H. Blanchard, Joy Belle Burgess, Sandy Cayman, Joan Donaldson, Beth Edwards, Llewelyn Evans, Rosalyn Hart Finch, Keith H. Graham, J. Harold Gwynne, Nelle Hardgrove, Clay Harrison, Glenda Inman, Jewell Johnson, Pamela Kennedy, Lucille King, Edgar Daniel Kramer, LaVerne P. Larson, Edith W. Lawyer, Pamela Love, Ann Lutz, Peggy Mlcuch, Ardis Rittenhouse, Kenton K. Smith, Eileen Spinelli, Louise Weibert Sutton, Kristi J. West, Harriet Whipple, Carice Williams, and Gaye Jones Willis.

Scripture quotations, unless otherwise indicated, are taken from King James Version (KJV). Scripture quotations marked NIV are taken from the HOLY BIBLE, NEW INTERNATIONAL VERSION®. Copyright © 1973, 1978, 1984 Biblica. Used by permission of Zondervan. All rights reserved.

Every effort has been made to establish ownership and use of each selection in this book. If contacted, the publisher will be pleased to rectify any inadvertent errors or omissions in subsequent editions.